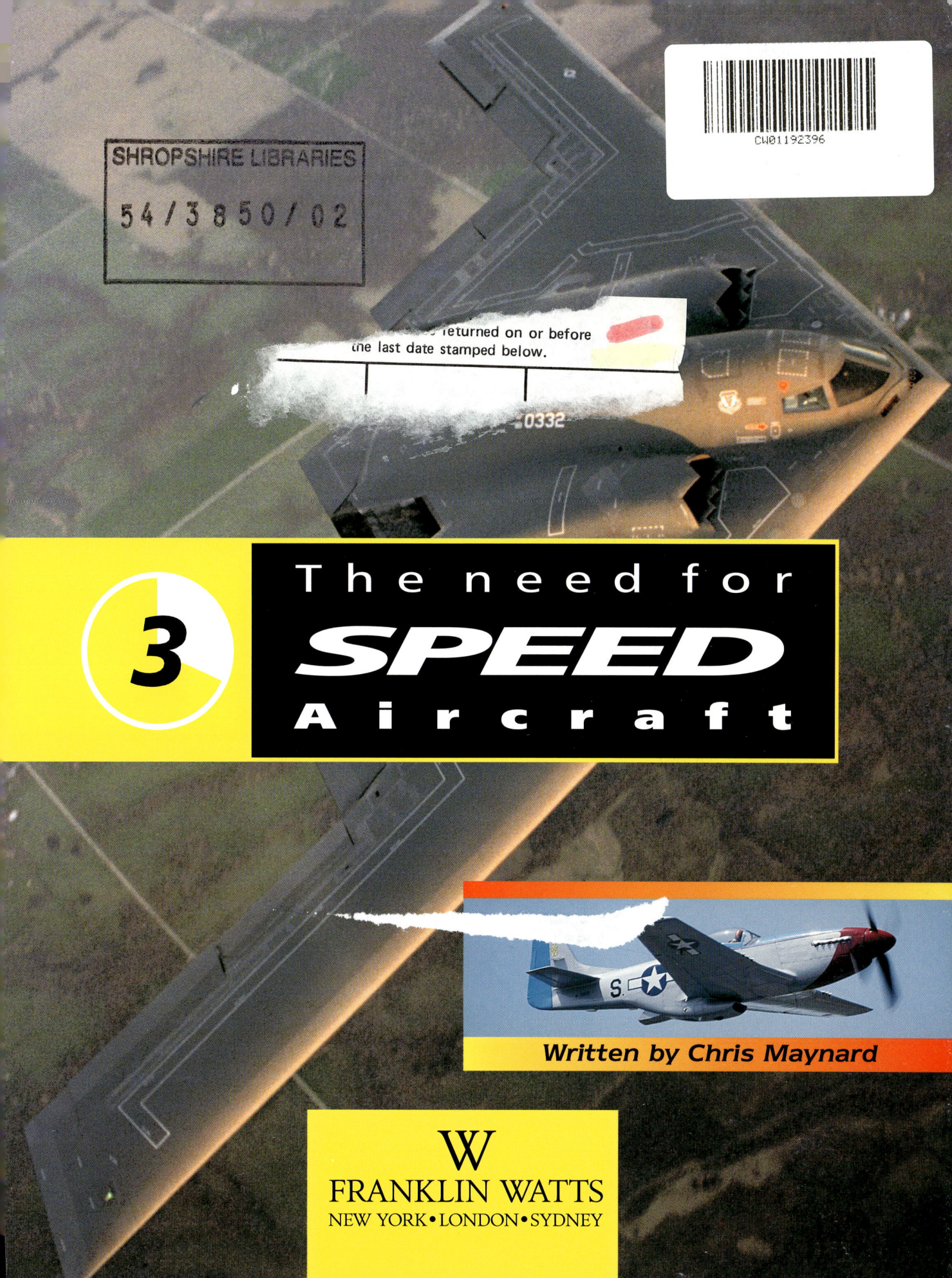

SHROPSHIRE LIBRARIES
54/3850/02

The need for SPEED Aircraft
3

Written by Chris Maynard

W
FRANKLIN WATTS
NEW YORK · LONDON · SYDNEY

CREDITS

This edition published in 2000 by Franklin Watts
96 Leonard Street
London EC2A 4XD

Franklin Watts Australia
14 Mars Road
Lane Cove
NSW 2066

© Franklin Watts 1999

Text: Chris Maynard
Series editor: Matthew Parselle
Designed by: Perry Associates
Art director: Robert Walster

A CIP catalogue record for this book is available from the British Library

ISBN   0 7496 3162 7 (Hb)
        0 7496 3915 6 (Pb)
Dewey Decimal Classification 797.5
Printed in Dubai

Picture credits: Cover: Front top – Aviation Picture Library (APL)/Austin J Brown; front middle and back inset – NASA; front bottom – APL/Austin J Brown; back – APL/Austin J Brown; Blackbird – APL/Austin J Brown; Quadrant Picture Library/Erik Simonsen; F-117 – APL/Austin J Brown; B-2 – APL/Austin J Brown; Quadrant Picture Library/Erik Simonsen; MiG-25 – APL/Austin J Brown; Quadrant Picture Library; APL/Austin J Brown; Tu-95 – APL/Austin J Brown; Quadrant Picture Library; P-51 – APL/Austin J Brown; Lynx – APL/Austin J Brown; Concorde – APL/Austin J Brown; Quadrant Picture Library; X-15 – APL/NASA; APL/Austin J Brown; NASA; Space Shuttle – NASA; Learning to Fly – Quadrant Picture Library; Quadrant Picture Library/R Shaw; APL/Austin J Brown; Stunt Planes – APL/Austin J Brown; Quadrant Picture Library/Nigel Jones; Quadrant Picture Library/R Shaw

CONTENTS

- 4 – 5 INTRODUCTION
- 6 – 7 BLACKBIRD
- 8 – 9 F-117 NIGHTHAWK
- 10 – 11 B-2 SPIRIT
- 12 – 13 MiG-25 FOXBAT
- 14 – 15 Tu-95 BEAR
- 16 – 17 P-51 MUSTANG
- 18 – 19 LYNX
- 20 – 21 CONCORDE
- 22 – 23 X-15 ROCKET PLANE
- 24 – 25 SPACE SHUTTLE
- 26 – 27 LEARNING TO FLY
- 28 – 29 STUNT PLANES
- 30 USEFUL CONTACTS
- 31 TECHNICAL TERMS
- 32 INDEX

INTRODUCTION

If you've ever wanted to know what it feels like to fly some of the most powerful aircraft in the world then The Need for Speed will let you in on the secret.

This book features an incredible range of airborne technology. Sneak a look at other countries' top secrets in the supersonic spy plane, the Blackbird. Snarl around a desert race course in a World War 2 relic, the P-51 Mustang, as you battle against other pilots in the 'world's fastest motor sport'. After all that, why not relax in luxury aboard the world's fastest passenger plane, enjoying a leisurely meal as you zip along faster than a rifle bullet.

As well as the thrills and spills, we also give you the facts and figures of these incredible machines. For every type of aircraft featured there is a Stat File and a Fact File.

The Stat File is a list of basic statistics about each aircraft.

This line tells you which type or model of aircraft is being looked at.

These lines give details about such things as length, wingspan and top speed.

The technical terms used in this book are explained on page 31.

STAT FILE

MiG-25 Foxbat

Length	24m (79ft)
Wingspan	14m (46ft)
Top speed	3000km/h (1875mph)
Power	2 turbojets
Crew	1 pilot
Numbers	Over 1200 built

The Fact File gives a slightly unusual, strange or funny bit of information about the aircraft.

FACT FILE

In the air, a Foxbat can point straight upwards and climb like a rocket up to about 24,000m (78,000ft). But from a standing start on the ground, it is beaten by the Harrier jump jet. A Harrier set a world record once by climbing to 12,000m (40,000ft) in just a shade over two minutes.

5

BLACKBIRD

If you spy on somebody and want to get away with it, try to make sure no-one sees you. But if you are seen, make sure you don't get caught. That's how the Blackbird did its job.

The Blackbird was a super-fast spy plane. The USA used it to sneak a look at secrets other countries wanted to hide. There was no way of stopping it because the Blackbird zipped along three times faster than a jumbo jet and flew over twice as high. Due to its speed, nothing – plane nor rocket – could shoot it down. And because it flew so high, its cameras had enormous views. They snapped photos of thousands of square kilometres of countryside an hour.

Tail Fins

Engines

Strangely enough the sleek, sculpted body, or fuselage, had no tail. But there were two tall fins on top of each giant engine that helped steer the plane in a straight line.

The wings were knife-thin and the engines were almost as fat as the body. As the Blackbird landed, it came in so fast it needed a tail chute to slow it down.

STAT FILE

Blackbird SR-71A

Length	33m (107ft)
Wingspan	17m (55ft)
Take-off weight	77,000kg (170,000lbs)
Engine	Two J58 turbojets
Crew	2 - a pilot and a systems operator
Speed	Mach 3.2 - 3400km/h (2100mph)
Max height	26,000m (85,000ft)
Range	4669km (2900 miles)

FACT FILE

The speed of sound as it travels through air is called Mach 1. It is a number that changes depending where you measure it. Down at sea level, Mach 1 is 1216km/h (760mph). In the high, thin air where jets fly best, Mach 1 falls to 1072km/h (670mph).

F-117 NIGHTHAWK

Armies use radar to warn of approaching enemies. But if an attacking plane reflects no radar signals then it cannot be seen. That's why the F-117 Nighthawk is called a 'stealth' aircraft. It can sneak up on targets undetected by radar. You only find out about it when it's overhead and dropping things on you.

The body of the dart-shaped Nighthawk is built from unusually shaped panels that are set at odd angles. Its surface is painted with a special dark material. The air inlets and exhausts hide the jet engines, and its weapons are deep inside the body. As a result, this fierce-looking fighter soaks up or scatters most of the radar signals that strike it.

The Nighthawk, the first stealth plane in the world, was first flown in 1982. It was built for the US Air Force in secrecy and was used with great success in the Gulf War of 1991.

Many attack planes rely on speed for safety. Since the Nighthawk is invisible to radar, it can fly fairly slowly without fear. This helps a lot if you want to drop bombs accurately.

The Nighthawk drops laser-guided bombs that can steer themselves right onto a target. From 7600m (25,000ft) it can hit objects as small as a table top.

All the edges of the plane have sawtooth patterns that scatter radar. There is not a single flat surface or right angle that radar can see easily.

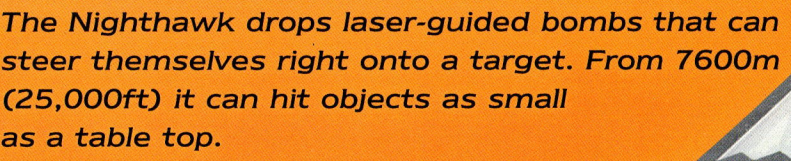

STAT FILE

F-117 Nighthawk

Length	20m (66ft)
Wingspan	13m (43ft)
Take-off weight	24,000kg (52,500lbs)
Crew	1 pilot
Top speed	Around 1100km/h (700mph)
Range	6230km (3894 miles)
Power	2 turbofan engines
Weapons load	Up to 2300kg (5000lb) of bombs

FACT FILE

The Nighthawk reflects about as much radar as a seagull. To an operator on the ground, a squadron of these planes looks like a flock of birds - not much to worry about at all!

9

B-2 SPIRIT

The B-2 Spirit is a long-range stealth bomber. It might look like a giant bat, but its strange shape means it is just as 'stealthy' as a Nighthawk (see pages 8-9). Although it is a huge plane, it can tip-toe past enemy defences easily to reach heavily guarded targets. Not bad for something as wide as a football field!

Unlike most planes, the B-2 has no tall tail-fin and no telltale engines slung under its wings. The whole plane looks like a great wing with rounded bulges on top, and a back end curved like a double 'W'. Its pilots boast it reflects about as much radar as a butterfly.

The surface of the plane is coated with the same special material as the Nighthawk. It soaks up radar waves like a sponge rather than reflecting them back like a mirror.

The Spirit's four powerful engines are buried deep inside the central part of the wing to make it harder for heat-seeking sensors to spot them.

The B-2 can range across oceans on its own, but if it is refuelled in mid-air it can reach just about anywhere from its home base in America.

It can carry up to 18,000kg (40,000lbs) of bombs or nuclear weapons.

Engines

STAT FILE

B-2 Spirit

Length	21m (69ft)
Wingspan	52m (172ft)
Take-off weight	153,000kg (336,500lbs)
Top speed	Around 1100km/h (700mph)
Max height	15,000m 50,000ft
Range	9600km (6000 miles)
Power	4 turbofan engines
Crew	2 pilots (with room for a third)

FACT FILE

The B-2 Spirit first went into service in 1993. They cost so much to build the US Air Force can only afford about 20 of them. Each one has a price tag of $1.3 billion.

MiG-25 FOXBAT

Some fighter planes are great at dog-fighting. They are nimble but not all that fast. Other fighters can fly like the wind to run down intruders and knock them out of the sky. They are called interceptors. The MiG-25 Foxbat is this second kind of plane.

It was one of the fastest fighters ever built, and it gave the US Air Force nightmares for a long time. It was Russia's answer to the fast, high-flying planes the Americans used to spy on what the Russians were up to. Only, it could climb much faster and outrun just about any fighter plane the USA owned.

FACT FILE

In the air, a Foxbat can point straight upwards and climb like a rocket to about 24,000m (78,000ft). But from a standing start on the ground, it is beaten by the Harrier jump jet. A Harrier set a world record once by climbing to 12,000m (40,000ft) in just a shade over two minutes.

STAT FILE

MiG-25 Foxbat

Length	24m (79ft)
Wingspan	14m (46ft)
Take-off weight	36,200kg (80,000lbs)
Top speed	3000km/h (1875mph)
Max height	24,400m (80,000ft)
Range	1700km (1060 miles)
Power	2 turbojet engines
Crew	1 pilot
Numbers	Over 1200 built

The Foxbat has two huge turbojet engines. Their brute strength can take the plane up to a blistering three times the speed of sound in a short dash. There is only one problem. If a pilot is not very careful with the throttle it is easy to run the engines so fast they destroy themselves.

The Foxbat has a single pilot who flies, navigates and fires the plane's missiles.

This scorchingly fast plane is also used for reconnaissance work. It can fly by, high and fast, to take a peek at something and then beat it before any other fighters get close enough to attack it.

TU-95 BEAR

The power of a propeller plane is no match for a jet. As a 'prop' plane goes faster, the tips of its whirling blades reach supersonic speeds. At this point, their pulling power drops off and the plane can go no faster.

Most propeller planes have a struggle to get up to 650km/h (400mph). But not the Russian Bear. The Tu-95 Bear is a big, long-range bomber that can race along at 920km/h (575mph) when it has to. That's over 80% the speed of sound. Although nobody has ever timed it, it probably holds the unofficial speed record for a propeller plane.

The Bear has a long, slender body and swept-back wings. Each of its four powerful engines drives two propellers that rotate in opposite directions.

Although it is built to carry bombs and missiles, the Bear has been used for long-range sea patrols for over 30 years.

All Tu-95 planes carry a long nose probe so they can refuel as they patrol.

The big bulge on its chin is a radar to help it navigate and watch the movements of other planes. Any bombs or missiles are carried inside the fuselage.

Radar

STAT FILE

Tu-95 Bear

Length	49m (160ft)
Wingspan	51m (167ft)
Take-off weight	188,000kg (414,000lbs)
Top speed	920km/h (575mph)
Max height	13,400m (44,000ft)
Range	12,500km (7500 miles)
Power	4 turboprop engines
Crew	7
Weapons	11,400kg (25,000lbs) of cruise missiles, air-to-surface missiles or bombs

FACT FILE

The strangest thing about the Bear is its contra-rotating propellers. This means that each huge engine drives two sets of props — the first rotating one way, the second the opposite direction. This is the secret of its incredible speed and power.

P-51 MUSTANG

Half a century ago, American P-51 Mustangs roared around the Pacific Ocean and the skies of Europe locked in combat with enemy planes. Almost 15,000 were built. Today, the last of these ageing fighters are still not gracefully retired. Far from it. They spend their time snarling around a race course in the American west.

At the Reno Air Races, in Nevada, old Mustangs and other planes chase each other around a circuit for the honour of flying faster and lower than anyone else. That means treetop-level flying at six times the speed of a fast family car. Not for nothing are these races called the 'world's fastest motor sport'.

The big Merlin aero engines have been tweaked and tinkered with to deliver 3000 horsepower, rather than the already impressive 1695 horsepower that made them some of the most powerful of World War II.

The wings have had a metre or so chopped off the ends to help the planes go faster.

The cockpit canopies are cut down and lowered, too, to make the old fighters more streamlined.

The Reno Air Races last for a week in September every year. Races follow one after another from morning until late afternoon. In between are displays of low-level aerobatics, assault parachute jumps, flybys of modern military fighter jets and precision flying shows.

Planes race over a 14-km (nine-mile) lap, and the final race is some 103km (64 miles) long. Winners clock up speeds rising towards 800km/h (500mph).

STAT FILE

P-51 Mustang (racing modified)

Length	10m (32ft)
Wingspan	11m (37ft)
Take-off weight	5454kg (12,000lb)
Crew	1 pilot
Top speed	690km/h (435mph)
Range	1600km (1000 miles)
Engines	1 Rolls Royce engine (3000 hp)
First flown	1943
Weapons load	6 machine guns with ten rockets or 900kg (2000lbs of bombs)

FACT FILE

In World War II, Mustangs were used to escort bombers on raids into Germany. They were spectacularly good at their job and by the end of the war had downed 4,950 enemy planes. This was more than any other fighter of the war.

LYNX

Speed does not come naturally to helicopters. They are built to fly slowly. One of the best things about them is the way they can hover at zero speed. But sometimes helicopters need to hustle. In wars, or rescue work, getting there fast is everything.

The Lynx is a fast and powerful military helicopter. It is used by navies and armies all over the world to hunt submarines, attack ships or ferry troops in and out of battle. It has a crew of two, except on rescue missions when a third crew member travels along to help survivors.

The world speed record for helicopters was set by a Lynx fitted with special, high-speed rotor blades. It flew faster than a Formula 1 racing car can drive as it hit 402km/h (251mph).

The Lynx runs on two turbine engines and has a rotor with four blades. This is how it gets its amazing power and speed.

The tail rotor keeps the craft pointing in the direction the pilot wants to go. Without it, the whirling of the big main rotor would make the helicopter spin in circles.

Lift is the force that keeps planes in the air. But when a helicopter flies too fast, its blades stop creating lift for part of their sweep. The helicopter bucks and vibrates. If the pilot doesn't slow down at once it will start to drop.

In search and rescue work, a special hoist is fitted by one door. It can haul two people at a time out of the sea or up from the deck of a ship.

STAT FILE

Lynx

Length	1.5m (49ft) includes turning rotors
Take-off weight	5330kg (11,726lbs)
Crew	2 pilots and up to 9 passengers
Top speed	400km/h (250mph)
Range	685km (424 miles)

FACT FILE

In 1994, a Bell Jet Ranger set a round-the-world record by helicopter. The crew flew 10 hours a day, made 84 stops and arrived back where it started after 24 days. The longest leg over water was the 700km (435 miles) hop from Labrador to Greenland.

19

CONCORDE

If you go on holiday across the Atlantic Ocean, the fastest plane you can travel on is Concorde. As you relax in luxury (it is all first class), you will find yourself speeding along faster than a rifle bullet with not a care in the world.

Concorde is the only supersonic passenger plane there is. It is a long, sleek machine with a pointed noise and wide wings, and it zips from London to New York in just 3 hours and 40 minutes. It flies over twice as fast and twice as high as all the jumbos and other big body jets plodding far below.

Only 16 were ever built, so Concorde is quite a rare thing to see if you ever go plane spotting.

Concorde flies at 18,300m (60,000ft). Temperatures at these heights are icy cold, yet the plane squeezes through the air so quickly the nose of the craft heats up by more than 140°C (300°F). The air is still hot enough to boil water as it flows past the plane. But inside, passengers notice this only as a cosy warmth radiating from the windows.

Concorde's nose blocks the pilot's view of the runway at landing and takeoff. So he lowers it to see where the plane is going. As Concorde climbs, he raises the nose straight ahead again for high speed.

FACT FILE

Concorde gets so hot from flying faster than sound, that the metal of its body expands. By mid-Atlantic it is 20cm (8in) longer than it was on the ground.

STAT FILE

Concorde

Length	62m (203ft)
Wingspan	26m (84ft)
Take-off weight	181,000kg (400,000lbs)
Crew	2 pilots and up to 100 passengers
Top speed	2179km/h (1362mph)
Range	6230km (3894 miles)
Engines	2 x Olympus turbojets

As there is no time for a movie during the flight, passengers get a long, delicious feast instead. By the time the last cups of coffee are cleared away, the plane is getting set to land.

21

X-15 ROCKET PLANE

Before space shuttles, or rockets to the Moon, there was one plane which could fly into space by itself. The US Air Force called it the X-15 (the 'X' stood for experimental).

During the 1960s, this rocket plane flew higher and faster than anything else in the world. It flew so high there was no air anymore for its wings to grab hold of. Instead, the pilot used 12 tiny jets in the plane's nose and wing tips to steer up and down and from side to side. Flight after flight, it climbed a bit further until it reached the height of 107km (67 miles). Because space begins about 80km (50 miles) up, at least half the X-15's test pilots earned themselves astronaut wings.

The X-15 flew to the edge of space and back. It climbed so high it left 99.9% of the Earth's atmosphere below it.

Its engine did not breathe air like a normal jet plane. Why? Because at that height, jet engines sputter and conk out. That high, there is not enough air to keep the fuel alight.

FACT FILE

The X-15's most famous pilot was Neil Armstrong, who went on to land on the Moon.

Most of the X-15 was a great big fuel tank with stubby wings on the sides. It had a rocket motor at one end and just enough room up front to squeeze in a pilot.

Wings

STAT FILE

X-15 Rocket Plane

Length	16m (52ft)
Width	6.7m (22ft)
Launch weight	23,000kg (51,000lb)
Rocket engine	26,000kg (57,000lbs) thrust
Fuel	8164kg (18,000lbs) of rocket fuel
Numbers	3 were built
Crew	1 pilot/astronaut
Top speed	7274km/h (4546mph) or Mach 6.3

The X-15 could travel at incredible speeds – over six times the speed of sound. To give you some idea of how fast this is, you would have to drive a car non-stop for three days and nights down a motorway to get as far as an X-15 went in an hour.

At the start of a flight, the plane was lifted a few miles up under the wing a of a B-52 bomber. Then it was released and flew under its own steam. The trick of starting at this height saved lots of fuel.

To save weight, and to make the craft as fast as possible, the X-15 had no wheels. Instead, it landed on metal skids and simply skied to a stop.

23

SPACE SHUTTLE

Planes fly in air. Rockets drill through it. The difference between the two is that planes have wings and can glide.

But the Space Shuttle does both. When it takes off, it flies like a rocket with its main engine and two booster engines thrusting it up into space. After two minutes of climbing it drops the boosters. After eight minutes, its big fuel tank falls off. Several days later, on the way back down, it flies back to Earth like a glider. It can't use the rocket engine now, but its wings and tail are enough for it to turn and steer. It finally lands on a runway, just like a passenger jet.

The Shuttle is covered all over with ceramic tiles that can withstand the searing heat as it speeds back into the atmosphere. If it was built out of metal, like a plane, the Shuttle would simply melt.

At launch, the Shuttle has four parts: a big fuel tank, two booster rockets and the main craft known as the orbiter. Only the orbiter comes back from space.

The orbiter has a deep cargo bay big enough to park a bus inside. It carries satellites and other scientific equipment up into space.

The Shuttle orbits Earth about 300km (186 miles) up and at a speed fast enough to cross the USA from coast to coast in ten minutes.

The crew live in a small cabin complete with flight deck, beds, kitchen, wash basin and toilet. There's no privacy here.

24

STAT FILE

Space shuttle

Length	37m (122ft)
Wingspan	24m (78ft)
Launch weight	77,000kg (170,000lbs)
Fuel	Liquid hydrogen and liquid oxygen
Crew	2 pilots and up to 5 passengers
Top speed	27,700km/h (17,300mph)

FACT FILE

The names of the four craft in the Space Shuttle fleet (Columbia, Discovery, Atlantis and Endeavour) come from famous sailing ships used by explorers long ago.

LEARNING TO FLY

Before a new pilot is let loose on a big expensive jet, he goes to school on something a little bit slower and lot less powerful. A jet with trainer-wheels, in other words.

One popular trainer is a quick little plane called the Hawk. It is a two-seater with a raised rear cockpit where the instructor sits. From back here, looking over his pupil's head, he teaches the new pilot how to fly a jet. The instructor has his own set of controls in case the pilot makes a mistake.

The biggest task is not flying the plane, so much as all the chores that go with it: navigating, defending yourself from attack, finding targets and firing weapons. One thing for sure - there's never time to get bored flying a jet fighter.

STAT FILE

Hawk Jet Fighter

Length	12m (39ft)
Wingspan	9m (29ft)
Take-off weight	5000kg (11,000lbs)
Top speed	1454km/h (909mph)
Range	2400km (1500 miles)
Power	1 turbojet engine
Crew	2

FACT FILE

For emergencies, a pilot has to learn how to use the ejector seat. The latest rocket-powered seats blast out of the cockpit four times faster than a jet takes off from an aircraft carrier. That's about 14 times faster than a Porsche 911 goes from 0–100km/h.

The new pilot learns to fly by sight and by instruments, so he can take to the sky at night or in foul weather without getting lost or confused.

The students learn to use the plane's weapons to attack targets on the ground and in the air. They also master the computers that control navigation, weapons and air defence.

Instead of having to glance around at banks of dials, the computer displays all the information a pilot needs straight up in front of him. Like this, he can use the plane's weapons without ever having to take his eyes off the sky.

The Hawk jet is used to train pilots in air forces all over the world.

STUNT PLANES

Planes performing stunts at high speed are very exciting and popular all over the world. The US Air Force has The Thunderbirds who fly F-16 fighter jets. The Swedes have Team 60. Canada has The Golden Hawks, and the Brazilians have The Smoke Squadron. The Red Arrows are one of the most famous stunt teams. They belong to Britain's Royal Air Force and have nine planes in all. Since the Red Arrows were formed, back in 1965, they have flown at thousands of air shows, fairs and public events around the world. At the last count, they had staged their show in front of millions of people in over 50 countries.

Thunderbirds

People are always thrilled by the team's high-speed rolls, loops and displays of precision flying. This kind of skill takes months of practice. The Red Arrows spend all winter preparing the 20 or so patterns they fly at each event during their busy summer season.

The trade mark of the Red Arrows is a Diamond Nine formation. It takes great skill to pilot each plane in a precise spot to create the diamond shape.

Flying beneath a blanket of cloud makes the planes sound much louder and appear much closer than when they fly in a bright blue sky.

For a full looping show, the bottom of the clouds must be over 1400m (4500ft) high. Otherwise planes vanish at the tops of their loops and the crowd below loses sight of the dramatic spectacle.

The planes never fly less than 300m (1000ft) over a crowd, but in front or to one side of it a pair of Red Arrows may fly past as low as 30m (100ft).

STAT FILE

The Red Arrows

Team	9 pilots
Management	10th pilot is the manager and show commentator, his plane comes along as a backup
Tour of duty	3 seasons with the team
Display	Over 20 different rolls, loops, corkscrews and patterns make up a typical display
Team trade mark	Diamond Nine formation
Training	All pilots have had one tour of duty with fast jets before they can join. Most are Flight Lieutenants in their late 20s or early 30s.
Equipment	Since 1980, the team has flown Hawk jets (see pages 26-27).

FACT FILE

Each plane has a tank of diesel fuel under the fuselage. When it is squirted into the hot jet exhaust it boils away as a thick trail of white vapour. If the pilot flicks a switch on the steering column, he can add red or blue dye to the vapour trail.

USEFUL CONTACTS

If you want to find out more about any of the aeroplanes mentioned in this book, here are some names which might be useful.

UK

48th Fighter Wing Heritage Park
RAF Lakenheath, Brandon
Suffolk IP27 9PN
Tel: 0138 523 000
A chance to see some of the most modern fighter planes.

Brooklands Museum
Weybridge
Surrey KT13 0QN
Tel: 01932 857 381
For vintage planes.

Imperial War Museum
Duxford Airfield, Duxford
Cambridgeshire CB2 4QR
Tel: 01223 835 000
The biggest and best collection of planes in the UK.

International Helicopter Museum
The Airport, Locking Moor Road
Weston-super-Mare
North Somerset BS24 8PP
Tel: 01934 635 227
Helicopters from all over the world.

Museum of Flight
National Museum of Scotland
East Fortune Airfield, North Berwick
East Lothian EH39 5LF
Tel: 01620 880 308
A huge and varied collection.

Red Arrows web site:
www.deltaweb.co.uk/reds
For details of their history, their planes, and their display dates for the year ahead, plus loads of facts and pictures.

Royal Air Force Museum
Grahame Park Way, Hendon
London NW9 5II
Tel: 0181 205 2266
A huge collection of planes, flown both by the air force and against it.

Science Museum
Exhibition Road
London SW7 2DD
Tel: 0171 938 8000
A terrific history from first principles right up to a sliced-through jumbo jet!

Shuttleworth Collection
Old Warden Aerodrome
Biggleswade
Bedfordshire SB8 9ER
Tel: 01767 627 288
British planes from the earliest days and World War 1.

TECHNICAL TERMS

There are some words in this book which you may not have seen before. Here is an explanation of them.

Air inlet: a hole at the front of a jet engine which allows air in.

Astronaut: a pilot who flies rockets or space shuttles into orbit around the Earth.

Bomber: a plane designed to carry a heavy load of bombs a long distance and drop it accurately onto a target.

Cockpit: the section of the plane that the pilot sits in.

Dog-fighting: a fight between two or more planes that chase each other around the sky, circling and looping trying to get into position to shoot the other one down.

Experimental Plane: a plane that is a one-off and is used to test body shapes or new engines. If large numbers of the plane are then built, it becomes known as a production plane.

Fighter: a plane whose main job is to attack other planes or to attack targets on the ground with rockets and bullets.

Fuel: liquid that burns inside an engine to make it run.

Glider: a plane that can fly without power.

Hover: when a helicopter hovers it hangs in one place in the air without moving forwards or back.

Jet Engine: an engine that burns a mixture of fuel and air (the air gets drawn into the engine by the blades of a big turbine) and blasts out hot gases that drive the plane forwards.

Jet Plane: a plane driven by jet engines instead of propeller engines.

Jumbo Jet: the very largest passenger jets, known also as 747s, are sometimes called jumbos because of their great size (Jumbo was the name of a famous zoo elephant).

Nose: the front tip of plane.

Propellers: the rotating set of blades at the front of an aeroplane engine that pull a plane through the air.

Radar: a system that uses radio waves to find planes and other objects. The waves bounce off the plane and and can tell radar operators how fast and in what direction the craft is heading.

Rocket Engine: an engine that does not need to breathe air but instead carries all its oxygen in tanks. Like this, it can travel through airless space.

Rotor Engine: the whirling blades of a helicopter are known as its rotor. Usually, there is one main rotor over the middle of the plane and one small one fitted sideways to the tail.

Runway: the flat, straight surfaces on which planes land when they come down.

Speed Record: the world speed record is the fastest speed for a plane of a particular type. A jet will have a different world record from a passenger plane or a helicopter.

Supersonic: faster than the speed of sound. Sound travels at around 1200km/h (750mph).

Throttle: a control that adjusts the power of the engine.

Thrust: the force that pushes a plane forwards at speed

Turbine: the series of spinning blades inside a jet engine. It may be used to drive the rotors of a helicopter, or to push hot gases out of an engine to thrust a plane forwards.

INDEX

air defence 26, 27
air temperature 20
America 10, 12, 16, 20, 21; see also USA
Armstrong, Neil 22

B-2 Spirit 10-11
B-52 bomber 23
Bell Jet Ranger 17
Blackbird 6-7
bombers 8-9, 10-11, 14, 17
bombs 10, 14

cockpit 16, 26, 27
Concorde 20-21
crew 18, 25

engines 6, 10, 13, 14, 15, 22, 24
    jet 8, 22
    Merlin 16
    turbine 18
    turbojet 13
    see also Stat Files

F-16 fighters 28
F-117 Nighthawk 8-9
fighters 8-9, 12, 16, 17, 26, 28
Foxbat see Mig-25 Foxbat
fuel 22, 23, 29
    tank 22, 24, 29
fuselage 6, 14, 29

Golden Hawks 28

Harrier jump jet 12
Hawk jet fighter 26
heat-seeking sensors 10
helicopters 18-19

interceptors

jet planes 7, 12, 14, 20, 22, 26, 27; see also engines, jet
jumbo jet 6, 20

learning to fly 26-27
long-range bombers 14
Lynx helicopter 18-19

Mach-1 7
Mig-25 Foxbat 12-13
missiles 13, 14

navigation 27
nuclear weapons 10

orbiter 24

P-51 Mustang 16-17
pilot 13, 18, 22, 26, 27, 29
propeller 'prop' planes 14
propellers 14, 15

radar 8, 9, 10, 14
reconnaissance 13
Red Arrows 28, 29
refuelling 10, 14
Reno Air Races 16
rockets 6, 12, 22, 24
    booster 22
    motor 22
rotor blades 18
rotor tail 18
round the world records 19
Russia 12

search and rescue 19
space 24
Space Shuttle 22, 24-25
Smoke Squadron 28
speed 6, 7, 13, 14, 16, 18, 22, 23, 24, 27; see also Stat Files
spy planes 6-7
'stealth' aircraft 8-9, 10-11
stunt planes 28-29

Team 60 28
Thunderbirds 28
Tu-95 Bear 14-15

USA 6, 8, 12, 24; see also America
US Air Force 8, 11, 22, 28

weapons 8, 26, 27
wings 6, 10, 14, 16, 20, 22, 24
World War II 16, 17

X-15 Rocket Plane 22-23